Liner Notes

Liner Notes

Poems by

Julia Knobloch

© 2025 Julia Knobloch. All rights reserved.
This material may not be reproduced in any form, published,
reprinted, recorded, performed, broadcast,
rewritten, or redistributed without
the explicit permission of Julia Knobloch.
All such actions are strictly prohibited by law.

Cover design by Shay Culligan
Cover image by Julia Knobloch

ISBN: 979-8-90146-600-1

Kelsay Books
502 South 1040 East, A-119
American Fork, Utah 84003
Kelsaybooks.com

Acknowledgments

Thank you to the following publications, in which versions of these poems previously appeared:

101 Jewish Poems for the Third Millennium: "Saint Lawrence River from the Plane"
The BeZine: "Arrival," "Pico-Robertson, Before Departure"
The Jewish Journal of Los Angeles: "Peaceful Dwellings," "Valley of Hinnom," "Ein Kerem," "Date Harvest," "Santa Ana"
Jewish Literary Journal: "Rehov HaMevaser"
Verklempt!: "Archaeology"

Contents

Deer Triptych	13
Soledad Canyon	16
Jerusalem	18
Mannheim Station	20
On Heiligenberg	22
Brothers	23
Ides of March	24
Rehov HaMevaser	25
Signal Hill	27
Sweetwater	28
Poem for a New City	31
Tidal Flats	32
3 Tammuz	33
passion and wrath	34
At the Cholla Cactus Garden	35
Route 90	37
Peaceful Dwellings	38
Phone Call	40
Cabo Raso	42
After the Lake	43
fragments	44
Brandenburg	46
Praia Grande	47
Genesee Avenue	49
Carthay Circle	50
White Faun with Flute	51
May Mirage	53
The End of December	54
Hippocampus Is Latin for Seahorse	56
Air India	58
Avenida da Índia	59

The Last Night in Buenos Aires	60
Venice	61
Saint Lawrence River from the Plane	62
Pico-Robertson, Before Departure	63
Palo Alto	64
Arrival	68
Valley of Hinnom	69
Archaeology	70
Ein Kerem	72
Pico Boulevard	74
Date Harvest	75
Memories of California	76
California Peaches	77
Santa Ana	78
Lines	79
Snow Day	82
Sunset Boulevard	84
Also I Return	86
Leaving New York V	88
Montauk Point	89
Double Eye	90
Kenneth Hahn Park	91
A Zimmer in the Forest	92
Tu BiShevat in the Arava	93
To Proclaim Freedom	94
Hiatus in the Sinai	96
Song at the Sea	97
Remember the Land	98
Under the Sun, Exactly	100
Prophecy Ceased	102
I Am Talking to You Now	104

Mount Royal	106
Ascent	108
Notes	111
Thank You	113

Deer Triptych

after poems by Georg Trakl

Placidity flows from the forest edge and
engulfs the trace back home
toward the shore behind the hills
where migrants once departed to traverse
rivers, canyons, and what lay beyond.

Some deer emerge at dusk.
From within the crimson now turned blue
unseen glances contemplate
four hundred miles and forty-four,
ten thousand years of inquiries.
Is the house by the bay unhurt?

Vigilant are the deer's warm eyes
they conjure threatened promises
while jugglers amble through the dark
blue woods; blackbirds and poets, too.

Don't break the spell.

*

The asphalt on the ramp has burst,
an animal has broken down and
perished at the curb.

Limbs stiffen, dull eyes perpetuate
tarred terror. A final wheeze hovers
unnoticed through the afternoon.

Cars rush past like saturated vultures,
brown bricks loom above frail structures.
Poppies poke through dusty cracks and
wane beneath a white, blind sky.

The bay is gray and dry
the house a sand-invaded ruin.

Land of Disenchantment.

*

Beams of light break through opaque air
rising murmurs fill the forest.
Perception blurs as evening approaches—
is it real?

Immobile, a deer stands by the wayside, staring
at beloved sounds: a flute, recitals
lost merriment.
O, speechless heart under satin skin!

Another step. One step too many or just enough
to shoo the luring spirits.
The deer flee trembling into hiding places
dissolve among green, gold and yellow faces.

The silence of the forest locks the magic.
In the clearing, an ancient grief bestows protection.
Late at night, the innkeeper turns off the lamp.

Infinity, almost visible.

Soledad Canyon

Between lost hills and dry ravines, a church
and an adobe house, a brick reservoir

Agua Dulce, Zanja Madre
mother of all aqueducts

In Sylmar, power winds down the mountain
like the fence between Eilat and Taba

like Mulholland meandering
past empty homesteads and lonesome oaks

like the pass snaking down to Sycamore Cove.
On the day after Yom Kippur, sheltered

by my open trunk door, I see ships land
and missiles fly—

Little have I changed although I contain
shards from all the places I have been.

I always hear the desert wailing, trains whistling
on arid tracks in the Sonora, an ocean

sweeping from the Kinneret to the Arava
where air and water taste of sulfur

danger hides across the border, landmines
and fault lines

shattered pitchers
at stolen cisterns in the valley, on US 395

Jerusalem

Maybe I have known you always because
you are the mother of all cities
mother of fire and mother of mercy
city at the edge of wilderness
city of jewels, eucalyptus and crows
of sniper-safe tunnels to heaven

Maybe because you are a fortress
heir to the crushed promise
to see a savior break through a walled-up gate
like rays of sun from the desert to your east

Maybe because I once fell in love within your borders
and now you are all that's left
with your graves on the Mount of Olives
stoic palm-trees
sweeping breezes that twirl windmill sails
like folk dancers
yellow ribbons flapping in the blue

Maybe I have known you always because
the Mediterranean is near
great sea of my youth
womb of my longings
at sunrise and sunset
where I first tasted figs and kisses

Now we are landlocked together, you and I
yet your terraced hills, your pines and cypresses
your crickets hiding in thyme bushes promise
that behind the next shrine
behind the next curve
there will be water

Mannheim Station

At Mannheim Station the world shrinks and expands, distance is relative to who we are. Decades ago, this station seemed a gateway to the world: tracks and dandelion, signal lights and switches; the teacher's command to walk in pairs, to not get lost; brakes screeching. It was the entry point back into safety, the local train across the platform, stale smoke in compartment wagons with brown and orange plush, summer skies heavy with dark-gray clouds behind the water tower. Our teacher pulled down the window, we fell asleep, uneaten apple slices in checkered knapsacks. Almost 10.000 kilometers from Mannheim Hauptbahnhof, a father talks with me about this railroad hub connecting east and west—or north and south—for a moment, he is not sure and I don't know, it doesn't matter, we share excitement for this port on the Rhine, cargo ships and alphabet streets, this bombed-out workmen's city, rebuilt ugly and confusing, with grand parks, green swimming holes. I want to mention that my father wrote his dissertation there and rode his Vespa through humid nights but then I don't, nor do I say I have a friend whose grandmother fled Mannheim as a child and that she looks like a local girl, girls I sat in classrooms with; nor that I wish my host could have changed trains there, too, after a field trip, on a visit to his parents, if this were possible; it's not, he would not be this man in California, weaving a map of Germany while his mother and his son observe in silence. I don't say that like him, like me, his son, my friend would not exist;

we came to life because others were forced in all directions, nor that I wish I could remain, talking, weaving, sheltered by two large candles behind me, in his house where his family has lived 35 years and some, nor that I wish I was a child again, a child who never left, who followed the command to walk in pairs, a girl who knows she's almost home when she arrives at Mannheim Station.

On Heiligenberg

To speak of curses that can befall our lives
do we ascend the mountain
to be close to the heavens and our fears
removed from valleys and from ghosts?

Do we go up because we need
another mountain
across the river
to absorb our words
to remind us
curses can be blessings
although we cannot see
the unrevealed in the revealed?

How do we know on which mountain
to build the altar and is that mountain
cursed or blessed
that it must be the place
where we pronounce
what once befell our lives
in a most splendid land?

On this holy mountain, facing the king's seat
how do I answer?

Brothers

You have been here before, turn around.

Have you forgotten the force of shared blood
of events before your time
when you don't count, never will?

It was never about you, you
who never tended goats in alpine valleys
who never saw the beach of Béjaïa
who never met the sisters and the mother
who always dyed her hair alone.
You never heard the wailing across the Méditerranée
you never knew the photo where he holds the silver spoon.

Have you forgotten
how fast a life was ended
how there was only silence and saliva on your cheek?

You can't fix the past by offering the same mistake again.
You won't know if they hate or love each other
but it is you who must leave, now.

Ides of March

The cherry trees were blooming, the air was humid, and the sun stood low as I led you to them in my orange dress. They waited for you with open arms.

My mother told you that they got to see the most wonderful sunsets from the deck, and how lucky we were tonight, with the wind dispersing the noise from the highway. Strands of hair streamed across her face.

My father pointed to the hills in the northwest, across the river, and patted your shoulder for lack of words. My brother gave me a wink and smiled at you in the evening's haze.

When the bells stopped ringing, you emerged from the shadows. You shamed my mother, choked my father, stabbed my brother.

I fell as quietly as a cherry blossom. In the meadow, my orange dress turned dark. The moon rose and the wind changed.

Rehov HaMevaser

Rehov HaMevaser runs above the valley
from where at first light
when sailors navigate by the horizon
the call to prayer rises

an ancient string instrument
a groaning, moaning
voices of sons and daughters
souls ascending from Gehenna
a storm that roars closer
thunder and lightning fill the void
between Abu Tor and Mount Zion
where steel cables were lifelines
deadly traps for helicopters

I am awake too early, exhausted
from releasing the woman
I thought I'd be in my year of jubilation

I stand by my window, behind the lattice
a barren and an unnamed mother
I cannot see
the splendor of Mount Zion
I cannot hear
the footsteps of the herald
Why so late, the echo of his heels?

Warm beams rise
over Silwan and concrete walls

cisterns and graves, the golden dome—

this land will not be tranquil as long as the sun shines

Signal Hill

I wanted to see Los Angeles and there she was
or rather her lights, far away—

the proud smile on my friend's face was the smile of a local guide
and as so often, I wanted to be a local, too.

I wondered if people here think of places as locations, this one
perfect for a breakup or first kiss, or something darker.

I wondered if I'd ever come up here again and not think of Vasco
in a morgue downtown on the night before his cremation,
if I'd ever come back to Los Angeles and when and why.

I remembered Signal Hill when I stood on a rooftop in Pico
with a different guide, this time by day.

We couldn't see Downtown, but we saw the mountains
and a church-like tower watching over a nearby park.

It is easy to find your bearings here, Noah said
and stretched out his arm:
You drive toward the mountains or toward the sea.

I looked across the canopy of palm trees
and it all made perfect sense.

Sweetwater

Tomorrow you'll be dead three years, and as always in early March, I visited your Facebook profile. I scrolled way back, wanting to find the you I had first met, and there you were, a photo I had never seen before. It hit me how young you were, sitting on the sofa in your mother's living room in Lisbon; me, a middle-aged woman staring at her past. I don't know why it hit me so hard, I have mourned you before; maybe because three years is enough time to begin to grasp the infinitude of death, maybe because of Ennio Morricone's soundtrack to "Once Upon a Time in the West" in my ears; I downloaded it just yesterday, and it stirred up something old, my dad in his morning gown, whistling on Sundays after breakfast, and only now did I recall that you, too, listened to that soundtrack a lot. *I hope you come back to Sweetwater someday,* I said when you left for the Film Institute in Los Angeles, and you answered, *Someday.* In the German version, dubbed, Harmonica answers, *Irgendeiner wartet immer, someone always waits.* I'm at LaGuardia, waiting to board a plane to Chicago on a business trip, in my ears the soundtrack from a film where a woman travels out west to unite with her husband who was just murdered by a gang of outlaws. This year began with you being killed in an accident on Beverly and Hudson and it ended with Leonard Cohen also dying in that sun-drenched city of patron saints, and it brought a lot of other losses, too, so I wrote a lot of poems and now my book is coming out and there are at least three poems about you in there. Every time I think of Chicago, I think of the fascination my father had for that city, a fascination that stemmed from a business trip he went on before my parents were engaged.

How proud he looked in his beige corduroy suit, with his sideburns, leaning against a railing in front of the Marina Towers; in a similar pose I remember you standing in front of the Kodak Theater which is now called the Dolby Theater. In Chicago, my father met with IBM, and in New York, he had meetings on Madison Avenue. It was an era when Europeans looked up to *America*, there still is awe in the way he articulates the word *Chicago*, in his thick accent. You had a very slight accent, that's because you went to an American high school, but there were a few idiosyncratic residues in your speech. I remember the Skype conversation we had, Skype, not Zoom, me shivering in a make-shift Tribeca office, exposed brick, telling myself and you that the unpaid internship with the famous filmmaker was going to be my foot in the door; you in a sleeveless t-shirt with your young son, a lemon tree in the background, telling him, *Say hi to Julia, she is in New York, where it's cold, look, she has a beautiful scarf wrapped around her neck*, in Portuguese you quickly threw in that I looked very pretty, and then you said, *New York still not working for you, hm?* I thought of your face when you walked up the stairs to your mother's apartment in Lisbon after your first year in the States. What have they done to him, I wondered, after only one year, Los Angeles not working for him. And now I have been here nine years, and you are dead three. You made it past one ocean and one continent, into the permanent MoMA collection and to two passports; you lost your life and your son and money and friends and something in your face that was still there when this photo on Facebook was taken. I earned my first dollars on a gig you had arranged for me, we were walking down Wythe, me in my famous red boots, and you said, *We immigrants must stick together,* and when we had burgers with the producer you smiled and said, *You are so fucking European,* because I used knife and fork, you said it with such warmth, and we all laughed. The producer didn't pay me as much as she had promised, but I never told you. So many things will remain untold. I don't know if Facebook will be around forever. I know the crevices of that sofa you're sitting on, and I know how that rug feels under naked skin and where the radio sat on the mantel. Maybe I always fall in love with film lovers because there's so much narrative potential in those connections. On this plane to Chicago, on the first day of Daylight Saving Time, I want to tell you that New York is working better for me now, better than it did when we walked down Wythe in the late September sunlight. I, too, have lost money and friends, my fertility, the beautiful scarf, and something that once was in my face, but I still have the same red boots I wore then and someday, I might come out west to Sweetwater. It will always wait for someone to come back, for immigrants like us.

Poem for a New City

The palm trees are not native, the driver says—
to me, they look as if they've always been here

like persimmons and pomelos heavy over hedges
holding secrets behind green screens—

the land where the citrons blossom
maybe it is here

light and shadow on scrubbed tiles
cypresses balancing on shaky

grounds of tar and oil.
Waves embrace me, hills invite me to ascend—

when I first came to this place, I paid tribute
to the dead; I could not un-

see magnolias beyond black mirrors
skies behind billowing curtains; I dreamed

of violet and pink flowers caressing
my cheeks and copper hair

of plantain trees that whispered, Touch me!
of one day returning for the sake of life.

Tidal Flats

We walk on the bottom of the sea
from one island to the next

barefoot through rippled mud and sandworm casts.
We must arrive before the night

before high tide
we must trust the guide when the moon is rising.

Glinting creeks are ocean in disguise.
Where are the sirens and the beasts,

where is the water?
How does it come back, seemingly
from below?

Hurry, says the guide. We must not see
the secrets of the sea, the margins of this earth.

A sailor binds, keeps watch—
we hear the leadsman calling.

The moon is red and close tonight.

3 Tammuz

to sink against you in the emptiness of 112 degrees—
my soul sighs like eucalyptus trees
at noon, mirage turns oasis
sublime lushness, shaded release

to kiss you in the silence of the desert
your strong slender arms
caress your face,
your hair's smell on skin and pillow
mingles with my sunscreen
now is our past and future
remember me for good

to be near you in this vastness, stars invisible
yet all around us, galaxies rooting and still
your heart remains not open
you say you want me to move on from you
i say your eyes are beautiful
you say it's beautiful to see my joy

let me say again, lovers can be vessels of salvation—
for the sake of our names
let us remember us for good
let us remember this earth house in the desert
to which we won't return, where you and i were one
one last time forever, on the day the sun stands still

passion and wrath

long ago, heat waves were nothing
but one endless summer
manifesting under naked feet
pearls of sweat on bronze
the smell of longing

how long it's been
and how much longer even
that i was a beloved's
no toy of lust misunderstood

in *La Piscine*
close-ups dissect shallow faces
tan in the stillness of Provence

now and again, i cut watermelons furious
with scorn and grief—
contrary to popular belief
there are ways to misread a poem

betrayal like the syrup from Ein Yahav
i brought home and let go bad

so many things i no longer do
seared into my being

At the Cholla Cactus Garden

We emerged from glowing magnetic fields—
nothing like the Milky Way to understand darkness

Blue and purple shooting stars coruscated
where one June, sterile light fell

on wrathful passion
watermelons smothered in date syrup
in a Mojave eucalyptus night.

Did they do it on the roof above my bed
in her car
or the white chairs by the firepit?

I dared one glance at that crimson soil of cruelty
waiting for the embers

to move out of sight as I steered south
toward the cacti and the cottonwoods.

I did not freeze, I was not alone. No need for selfies.
My friend sat on a boulder

the earth scrunched under our secure steps.
We had a map, the music of our youth. She said

it may seem that mountains never change
but they are not eternal, either.

What terrifying thought, yet oddly comforting
in the larger scheme of things.

In this wide basin of late sunlight, giving itself over
to the Colorado desert, waves carved rock

like reed grass waving in my mother's garden—
how she loved the reed grass in that garden

she had to leave behind. A thought that takes my
breath and sleep away. My friend knew. We knew

many things then in the silence, at the confluence
of two deserts, driving against the setting sun.

Route 90

The dusk tastes of sulfur, a flaxen breeze blows
from red mountains through Negev dwellings

Eden my wilderness, spring of salvation
Dates, olives, grapes—

on the kibbutz I learned each harvest has its own word
for separating fruit
from the cluster, the branch, the vine

Our songs echo over cooling sand, climb up
flanks of valleys descending into darkness
as the bus moves north

The day has gone, turned palm trees into silhouettes
white lights from cosmetics factories
advertise miracles through the night

The moon shimmers on the opaque sea
I see my mother at an alpine lake, waving
back at us from a distant platform
like in a silent movie, a recolored photograph—

loneliness passed on through generations

How I yearn to inherit this desert life
a sun-burnt patch of arid land
where I can sit and watch
the mountain colors change, clefts take shape
and wave at loved ones far away

Peaceful Dwellings

Journeys of reinvention, neighborhood of refuge
and cinema, where a poet's footsteps echo louder
than those of the redeemer

Squashed olives on the stairs that belong
to cats and brides and graduates
Water gushes toward the valley in cascades
of petals, pebbles
Windmill sails hover over puddles, blurring
the reflection from the wine bar's light bulbs

On Pele Yoetz Street, my father pauses and recalls
our first walk one week ago:
the synagogue we passed, the bench we sat on
the photo he took of his wife and daughter
fountains and children in the background
and David's tower

Nodding, he repeats out loud the names
of all that he may not return to see:
the sultan's pool, the mayor's park, the Turkish wall
days in a hotel on Hebron Road
room with a panoramic view

my mother on the bed's edge
mending my leggings' seams
my father on the other side stretched out

resting after hours of sun and stones
and I, child again between them
watching the sky embrace the Mount of Olives, Zion

Phone Call

They're going to Mannheim, my mother tells me, shopping, as one does, maybe a jacket for dad, for her a scarf, a pair of shoes; they'll stroll about as they have always done, reminisce about my father's college days, when Mannheim was the cosmopolitan choice, not Baden-Baden with its coffee-cake daintiness; they'll take the train, she says, driving is getting harder at their age; they'll step off the regional express onto the platform, breath like smoke from factory stakes in the December cold, shadows on beige station buildings in pale sun, my father adjusting his coat's collar, my mother's fingers freezing despite the leather gloves, frost on tree branches waving in front of the water tower

How many times have I written about my parents standing on a platform, looking for me among the just arrived, waving goodbye; walking with the train slowly pulling out, looking to find my face behind darkened window panes; these days, you can't pull down the windows anymore and wave for as long as you need, until you no longer see even a dot, until you're just waving to yourself, to the years left behind, to the landscape that will always smell familiar; wave like my grandparents at the curb with a handkerchief, until our car had turned the corner, until it was only my grandmother and then just us driving past the house where now, other people live

Always have breakfast, my father said, never go into debt; keep a bottle of water in the trunk and a small rag in the gloves department. I mostly adhered to his advice; for a while I even had leather gloves in my Renault 5, how proud gloves and first car made me, driving up to Mannheim, a milestone, an initiation, pulling out of the station, fading out of sight

Cabo Raso

On a cliff, I sit on your lap
your legs dangle in the void,
mine are locked around your hips,
below us secrets lurk in blue and white

Your curls in saltwater sunshine.

On a whim I bend backwards
until sky and sea flow into one
another and with open arms
I take in the world

Your curls in saltwater sunshine.

On Restelo beach, an old man
shakes his head and walks away,
mothers cry as ships sail down the river,
you speak to me, but I can't hear you

Your curls in saltwater sunshine.

After the Lake

Driving home from the lake—
bare feet on the pedals, dusty and dry,
scratches from nettles and little branches
on my legs but it doesn't matter,
because they are tanned

Driving home from the lake—
my hair an unruly bunch of curls
jumping up and down before my eyes
but I don't mind because the wind is fair

Driving home from the lake—
the village square is hot and empty,
the silence reminds me of singing crickets
and sighing wheat fields,
of a yellow towel billowing through the air,
of light that penetrates my eyelids
I smell of sweat, reed, and seed,
the sun burns down on my left arm and thigh

I love every inch of my body and life.

fragments

sand on my floor
light in slanted angles
on my sundress draped
over the closet door
i feel pretty because of you
don't want to shower, want to
keep the seed of Israel inside me
it is running down my thighs
want to keep your smell
in my salty hair
your fingertips behind my ears
venice was the closest
we've come to swimming
or was it santa monica
boundaries are blurry
fragments swirl like rip curls
again a circle closed
on the I-10
between great sea and hill country
joshua
they say your book
is not included in the Torah
yet brings fulfillment of God's promise
a fleeting sense of future—
this fog behind the bridge
this northern dusk
this wind over the bay
when all is said, or not
i will recall
your voice so close

the sand i patted from your face
the wonder that was tasting your lips again
the quietness of the world
green waves glittering behind us

Brandenburg

The pine needles had no scent, the fire risk was high,
a breeze of dry-cleaned clothes and sunscreen

blew through our car, a hazy sky,
the road to our friends' wedding, empty.

We stopped at a lake, jumped into opaque water,
the reed grass quiet in the afternoon, the soil light.

As a girl, I always wore a bathing suit under my dress,
ready to run barefoot over wooden planks and dive

into a lake, sunburns and splinters proof
for wisdom gained in endless summers.

They held the reception at a red-brick farmhouse owned by artists;
a goat on the roast, mattresses under linden trees, paper lanterns.

All night we drank only water.

Before I knew you, I knew arid mountains.
You taught me lushness, the use of sunscreen.

I have returned to my deserts, where I carry
your lakes inside me, your smile in strawberry evenings.

Praia Grande

Quando depois do sol não vem mais nada

I am ready, swimsuit under my blouse and jeans, I sit in the cafeteria, at a greasy plastic table cluttered with torn sugar sachets, pastry crumbs, ashtrays and used coffee glasses. Um galão, dois galões, try to say that when you're not Portuguese. You know where the Language Department is; your mother used to teach here. Early afternoon, the light so glaring it's almost black, you walk across the dusty concrete; you wear a Mano Negra t-shirt and you've brought an extra helmet. I can't take my eyes off you, even when you're standing right in front of me. You kiss my forehead and to my friends from class you wave hello. Where are we going? I could ask that in Portuguese, but we speak English. I'm taking you to Praia Grande, you say. We fly through alleys of swaying reed grass; up in the hills, near the Palace of the Seven Sighs, the air is cooler than in the city. Past sturdy vineyards, the road leads to the coast; I hold on tighter, because the curves are narrow and you take them fast, until the beach unfolds in front of us. The big beach, what better name for this endless stretch of sand and roaring, foaming water! Seagulls hover in the air, the skies of Lisbon in their eyes, watchful eyes, like the eyes of surfers, who stand immobile on a low stone wall, next to the man who sells bread with chouriço, that's where the charcoal smoke comes from; as high tide approaches, the wind is stronger than the sun, your hand in mine. You must be careful with your skin, you say, sand under my back and then shadow, the shadow of your face so close; your body is my sunscreen. Children yell, a baby cries, random bits of conversation left or right, a ball game, running feet, it all sounds very far away. I listen to your quiet voice and feel the first splashes of the nearing waves on my shins and on your back. We should move . . . yes, in a minute, soon . . . now the water has touched our toes, one toe, two tões! If we just had this beach for us alone in all its glorious, glistening blue and yellow; if all these people weren't here, too . . . who cares, they don't notice, yes, they do . . . maybe . . . no . . . if only . . . seven sighs . . . Cold and powerful, the tide glides over us, it's now impossible to tell between sweat drops and Atlantic dripping from your eyes, your laughing, marveling eyes that comprise the Lisbon skies and the seven seas and the notion that beyond the sun live tenderness and loneliness. T i m e

passed, you stopped calling, you never again took me to Praia Grande. One day though, by myself, I did return and there you were; you walked alone along the shoreline. You were surprised when I appeared in front of you, but you just smiled and kissed my forehead; your glance was distant, kind. Together we sat down and watched the tide, immobile like surfers, who read forever the bending and breaking of the waves.

Genesee Avenue

Afternoons are a smiling gecko daze
under blue and purple flowers that shower
my thick hair and yellow towel

hot stones in the patio recall childhoods
of garden hose and water sprinkler
fountains of iridescent mirth

the scent from citrus orchards
lingers like an apparition
of a distant homeland's shore
in this grove where the palm tree grows

a cactus blooms red against white walls
a spider dangles, leisurely
pomegranate branches swing shadows
over turquoise tiles, decades of lived love
dwell in this space

I wander barefoot past worlds of books
scout out the path of solstice sunlight

Come morning, another teeming day
takes shape outside, rising like song
from stones and grass that still hold on
to the cool warmth of night

Carthay Circle

On the first morning of Daylight Saving Time, we walk through the neighborhood, Aviva and I, spring is here and Los Angeles brimming, the hills are of an unseen green, the trees teeming especially giddy in pink and pink, the air unusually warm as was last night that held the jasmine in an extra-long embrace while the clocks were turned ahead, one hour lost, so many won—Aviva tells me how the city guards memories of generations although the tram no longer runs on San Vicente and the movie theater is gone but the name lives on and her grandparents' house was on this block and thirty years ago, she planted roses and tomorrow, purple iris and for a moment I forget my unpruned vineyards, barren fields—crows keep hopping and we keep talking and still the sun's not setting until eventually a whiff of evening touches our cheeks that beam like windowpanes of mansions in the canyons—a day inscribed into the breezy LA annals

White Faun with Flute

After the rain, the desert is a field of herbs
a rainbow behind the eucalyptus tree,
weeping willow of parched lands,
a saffron glow over the Airstream
dry soil and pinecones
the scent of my first perfume
Grasse-en-Provence
my first kiss under palm trees
indigenous to all exotic places—

Enchanted by the new-won knowledge
of my unfolding life
I kept the empty flask, Occitan mysteries
of ragged valleys, lavender hills
where a white faun played the flute
although the summer ended like a French movie—

Fifteen, tan and wild
lilies of the valley pulsing behind my ears
I cried at my mother's shoulder
my mother
who stroke my hair with knowing and introduced me
to *Pierrot le Fou* and *La Piscine*
to *À Bout de Souffle* and to *Jules et Jim*—

Life they say is not a movie, yet like a movie life
grows and unearths hidden threads
sudden scents and melodies
fleeting connections that are lasting

like on the last day of December
riding with a lost love's mother
in her son's hybrid car, in a city
where palm trees now are signs of home
holding the gift she gave me, a framed poster
Picasso's *White Faun with Flute*

She too knew Grasse and the Provence, French movies
she knew of sacrifices men will make for one they love
she knew pain and life, how *serious* it is
that there is no time to lose—

We walked, arms linked for a brief while
down Rodeo Drive and up a little hill
a faint song of miracles beyond its season. Tonight
in the Mojave, beneath oily eucalyptus trees
I remember our laughter, her gift on my wall, the distant city

May Mirage

89 degrees in Echo Park and 68 in Venice, in one hour
On Mulholland, the smell of warm soil at dark
cicadas buzzing in the parking lot, sparks on Electric Avenue
palm trees bending in a neon-purple breeze

Grizzlies walked on Abbot Kinney; camels roamed the grass
between La Brea and the beach, and horses
before they went extinct and then returned
aboard the Spanish ships

High tide rolls in, hills are melting in the Palisades—
no end-of-days sweet wine during the Pleistocene
but giant fern, and mammoths swimming to Santa Rosa Island
that floats veiled in moist air

In his house in Rancho La Ballona, a friend shows me a map
the land grants yellow, pink and purple
a wooded island in the creek
mission bell and fan palms, torch lilies and a Cessna plane

Where was LA when they found skeletons in bubbling asphalt?
Mud and derricks and the same mountain silhouette
no oranges, no studios, no Spanish revival
not even Third Street, where garbage twirls along the curb

The purple month of May is almost over
photos can't do the jacarandas justice
in real-life and from afar, they are brimful clouds
close-up they are gauzy, flimsy petals sprinkling
the sidewalks; the sunlight golden as 11000 years ago

The End of December

At four in the morning, beauty hides in silent streets
I used to saunter through such velvet vastness
and bring the sun into my house, as one who says
It is good
when entering an unfamiliar city
because God said so, too, in a beginning
Now the date palm, whom I love, looks sad
battered from the storm
her fronds, once perky like the righteous
are brown and droop
she bore no fruit this summer
and I stay to keep her company
while the dark blue turns purple
while my womb expires
unused compassion gushes forth
for days on end
while the year is fading out
God of Mercy
where are my childhood's hopping crows
and where is Joseph our brother now
and is the cockatoo in Venice still asleep
and is it jet lag, bitterness or grief
that wakes me up each night
and makes me wait for dawn?
Light peeks through cypresses and finds my face
Shout for joy, burst into song—
One more year and I am set to reap
fruits of my labor, in a place still unrevealed

I might leave this now familiar city, I might cut
bonds that never were, might say
It is good
because in the morning, the men were sent away

Hippocampus Is Latin for Seahorse

Indelible in the hippocampus is the laughter

I have been wanting to write a poem about memory shaped like a seahorse floating through turquoise waters. The English lacks the endearing tone of the German *Seepferdchen:* baby seahorse, little horse of the sea. Much of the #TooLong I stayed with my ex-husband can be explained with my belief in the peach pie heartland of this country. Once I was a young girl sitting in a living-room in West Germany, watching "Little House on the Prairie." My natural hair color has a tinge of auburn, but I wanted ginger braids like Melissa Gilbert's, bouncing up and down while she came running toward me through the prairie grass. "Little House on the Prairie" premiered on September 11, 1974, exactly one year after Salvador Allende killed himself during a savage US-backed coup d'état in Chile to save Latin America from communism. Indelible in my face is my ex-husband's fist; tank treads in vandalized backyards. I first heard of countries like El Salvador and Grenada on the eight o'clock news; I bought henna hair dye and fair-trade coffee from Nicaragua in what was then called Third World stores; I interviewed people tortured by condors and falcons. Now the marines are landing on the shores of Alta California, once again folks, and I wonder how Phil Ochs would deal with all this, the singing journalist. In Santo Domingo, the old women sigh, think of memories gone by. I learned how to scuba-dive off the shores of the Yucatán peninsula, I floated with manta rays and seahorses through turquoise waters. Once I was a redhead with curls. I lived in a house with a husband, we had a mobile of painted wooden fish and shells hanging in the bathroom. I imagined how one day it would spin over a crib while I would serenade the child, maybe a little boy, who would grow up eating peanut butter and jelly sandwiches, learn how to scuba-dive and play the guitar and stand up for what's right, my little ginger-haired American pioneer, my baby seahorse.

Air India

The old new day is a red and saffron-yellow ribbon
against the indigo arctic midnight—dawn in limbo
magnetic compasses are useless
The plane flies west toward the east
on lower altitudes to prevent fuel from freezing
My past selves look at me
from the point between my eyebrows
like the three heads of Shiva
like the photographs in my lover's bedroom
near the river, 25 years ago
He loved to capture the colors of India
my tan youth in black and white
You must go one day, he said
At 31, I stood on the shores of Mozambique and Muscat
overlooking what remained of da Gama's route
my hands painted with floral ornaments
my hair soaked with a warm breeze
framed by a red and saffron-yellow scarf
Now I am coming from the west the east the north
crossing Siberian plains, a glimpse of the Himalayas
leaving yet again uncharted
my waters of the Indian Ocean, the Arabian Sea

Avenida da Índia

We ran through the sprinklers on the lawn
in the Vasco da Gama Garden in Belém
named after the seafaring man who sailed to India.

We ran and laughed, and laughing we fell to the ground.
My blouse was checkered, blue and white
and then green, too.
I was in love with the smell of warm wet grass
with you.

Night was coming. Across the city, couples clung closer
on park benches or near the castle.
We had time, the temperature wouldn't drop for hours.

You took my hand and led me across the train tracks.
There were no overpasses then, only wooden planks
and warning signs:
Stop. Listen. Watch. One train may hide another.

Don't fall in love with me, you said, your profile
sharp against brightly lit heroes hewn in stone
down by the river.
Don't fall in love with me, because I don't know if I will.

The bridge sparkled in our backs, ahead the open sea.
I can't ask you anymore, I never did while I still could—
what difference did it make?
We both knew that you would leave for India.

The Last Night in Buenos Aires

It's four in the morning, an austral November—no, it's not, four in the morning, though it is the end of May; it has been getting colder since your letter, your absence feels more tangible with each day, since I first noticed it at the registry in Tribunales, where I searched for an Austrian writer's traces, his marriage license signed by an impromptu witness, hiding among names of millions of strangers, among them, I reckoned, you. There was music on Uruguay Street as I walked to the station, because I love the avenues I went to Callao, and at the corner of Paraná I looked up, hearing again your remarks about the here and the now, and when I saw the shutters still closed on the seventh floor, your absence turned presence, once more. When you left, I didn't know what you wrote me later, that someone was waiting for you in a distant home, that you were not sure where you belonged— in a house in the desert, the mountains or by the shore, that it tortured you how moving on felt like moving in circles, or back and forth. This past Sunday in Palermo, strolling through green, amber parks, your friend and I evoked the last night we saw you, how somber you looked, ready to embark, as you adjusted your hat in front of the mirror, while the piano was playing and the light here grew dimmer, and the sun swiftly rose over the Balearic coast.

Venice

The waves rumbled, the surf was foam,
we made it through the sea.
The coast regained serenity, palm trees quiver platinum
eucalyptus leaves are golden green, impossible to tell if real or
sparks in anthracite glazed mirrors, windows in wood panels.
The shower's rain engulfs my skin, my old new life
that I will leave behind.

Who can harvest all these oranges?

The bird on my shoulder has peach and scarlet feathers,
I cut up bananas, I whistle, I hide in plain sight
like women from bygone eras who sojourned in the countryside
to return with child, without a father.

I wait for blood that may not come again, for living waters.

When I first wrote about pebbles, dust and earth
under naked feet
on my path through lands not sown
I still believed a seed would grow
a father find ground water
a pomegranate flower.

Now I walk through the shadow of olive trees.

If I found a waterhole there in the mountains
would I enter, would it irrigate my soul like the first fig tree
I ate from, in Sanary, in 1993?

The sky tonight is blue and orange, a pool of sunken blessings,
in the rosemary-scented breeze
cockatoos raise papaya-colored crests

Saint Lawrence River from the Plane

for Leonard Cohen

The great river I wanted to see since I was twelve
streams below me to the north-east.

Thin ice floes swirl around the islands, past
silent reed grass and stiff poplars, the clock tower

on the pier. This is the birthplace of your poetry,
where tea and oranges touched your mind.

You taught me to lean out for love.
I lean against the window,

with the skyline, translucent smoke floats
over black-lit copper, charcoal, bronze, and white—

the only green, for one moment,
the bridge and lady of the harbor. And then

the holy mountain where you are, frozen earth.

Pico-Robertson, Before Departure

A back-alley glows in apricot and pink
seven trumpets praise the early sun

Crows sit on wires like purple sparks
palms worship the wind, their fronds clatter
like plastic blinds in a sparsely furnished bedroom

June gloom stretches into July, a skateboard
stumbles over rotten dates

Marine layer is just another term for fog
but the beaches in the west are always open

The hot months I love to greet will arrive
after I have traveled to a summer in decline

My peach garden will be gone when I return
others will harvest what they planted
sit on dunes and squint their eyes
watch the sun set behind mid-century balconies
contemplate desert colors from the snow

Now that the silent neighborhoods light up
again, I must leave
although I still don't know what happened
to the silver hoops I forgot
pool-side on Shenandoah
next to a pile of cherry pits, another layer of my soul

Palo Alto

Rain rain rain; if I were to make a movie out of that last weekend in Palo Alto, it would be an Italian movie, or a French one, but the Italians are more brutal in dissecting lust, cowardice, abyss, his lips my lips apocalypse, and had this been in fact a movie, we might have hurled stuff at each other or yelled curse words *outside,* which to him was a more horrendous scenario than treating me ruthless *inside* his charmless overpriced wall-to-wall carpeted 2BR, any rent peanuts for a Silicon Valley employee, because what would the neighbors think; but we stayed quiet *enough* and I grabbed my blue carry-on and turned around in the rain and walked to the Uber, my purple hoodie flooded when I arrived at SJC from where I called my friend, and I didn't care that I was crying because I for one am not squeamish about lamenting in public, I have watched my share of French and Italian movies to make up for the lack of Middle-Eastern blood running through my veins (although he conceded once that he would count me in a minyan); it's also true that one can't smoke in airports anymore in this country or anywhere in the world, which could have been another scene, the heroine leaning back detached and defiant in those blue plastic seats, blowing smoke directly into the camera while outside the rain is falling, the first of August and 58 degrees and although rabbis-to-be should not take an oath lightly, I vowed to never again set foot into this self-gratified town with its students strutting down sleek University Avenue that looks even more provincial than its sister city's pedestrian mall where people run up and down like hamsters all day every day and literally everyone looks white. Oh, these people here like money, he chuckled, referring to his salary, a sheepish young-ish man who after all will be pushing forty sooner than later at this point and will have more money on his bank account than I ever dreamed of making at forty, but I also would have never moved to Palo Alto for the life of me; rain this entire weekend, patches of sunlight here or there but only in the sky and in hindsight everything is gray and cold and bleak, like fog-and-rain covered Half Moon Bay, where other people go on honeymoons but now the beach was deserted except for a red ball on the wet brown sand, next to some kelp and wooden planks, and I took a photo of the ball while he pissed against the battered dunes, maybe it could be a sign of hope, the red ball in monochrome nothingness, but it only reinforced the loneliness, like Barbara's Fishtrap, where he let me choose Rice Pilaf, which admittedly wasn't very good, over the coleslaw he wanted and picked up the check, one shared fish filet in Vera Cruz sauce, one shared Rice Pilaf, not very good, and tap water; he was annoyed by my story about the days when I was younger than he ever was and filming in Oaxaca, which keeps showing up in my life in strange ways but I won't go into that now; he was not interested in hearing that I ate pescado à la Veracruzana every night in the bungalow hostel overlooking Puerto Ángel, the thick humid air making my skin shine and my hair curl, and my body was lean and tan, and there was a parrot, too, and I was hungry for life and love and the mysteries of remote places with little electricity, and at night the water in a halfmoon-shaped bay looked like one black diamond. Picking up a $26 check and buying three half-rotten avocados for $2 at a stand on PCH was all he was willing to invest, he couldn't pretend more interest because he knew I would misinterpret it as I had done over and over again before, though sleeping with me over and over again over years apparently did not count as interest, and so I just fell silent and looked over the bay and thought, Full Moon over Half Moon Bay, what a title for a poem, or should it be New Moon, I have forgotten what phase of the month I was in then anyway, that should tell you something, and now that we were walking over the parking lot where the gentiles stood drinking beer on a Saturday afternoon I wondered, not for the first time in my life, whether unrequited love is actually love, if I can truly love someone who never reached for me in the night, never wanted to see my smile in the morning and give me a kiss, deep and warm, like in a Leonard Cohen or Bob Dylan song, and beheld me, if only for one moment, rather than putting his full weight, no matter how skinny, no matter how brief, on my arm without looking at me and yes, in fact there *were* bruises on my arm, they only disappeared once I arrived in the Holy Land, but no, for the record, he never hit me, not in Palo Alto nor anywhere on the three continents where I helped him keep his hands ritually pure and yet, by the end of that last weekend I began to look *as if* he had, but duh, he wouldn't take accountability for that of course. What he did say on that last morning was, Oh, I'll have you walk to the station, the rain is not too bad; his demeanor more tensed than when he was racing back from No Moon Bay behind a dirty and fogged-up windshield, when I should have said, I don't even *like* you enough to want to die with you on the scenic 280, clean your windshield and stop texting and tell your dad,

No, Julia does *not* sleep on the couch, and tell whoever was on the phone earlier, Yes, *she* is still here, and right, right, why *am* I still here, but I didn't say any of that, or maybe I said, Please drive carefully, or maybe I prayed, Please let this be over, and it was so, although everything else I had prayed for over the past five years I had prayed for in vain, like a certain man, חַד גַּבְרָא, who prayed for a shidduch although the woman was not destined for him and when he got her he just wanted to get rid of her and that's why it doesn't make sense to ask for an impossible shidduch, to pray for something not meant to be—
 now what do you think, Godard and Antonioni?

Arrival

In the first week, sleep comes any hour, hunger early
when the pillar of dawn climbs up the stone wall
in gray and blue, and the neighbors have sex, again

In the space between jetlag and transition
exhilaration and exhaustion
water from the shower engulfs my skin
an orange glow
It seems easy to wash away age and memories
craving to emerge
to exhale, to play a wind instrument

With gusto, I eat olives and labneh, warm pita
with za'atar from the Bukharian baker
I can't write a line but walk far and beyond
in somnambulant serenity
through alleys that smell of fresh detergent
moth powder and worn ceramic tiles

I nod and smile and some smile back
I am not deaf but mute
I log my journey of discount and preparation

Valley of Hinnom

The hills of hell are green in spring, dotted
with plum and almond trees whose blossoms
cover scars, dug into muddy soil by bulldozers
slowly merging from both sides
Orange fences wind through the terrain
like salamanders, where in late summer
sunflowers turned their faces toward me
as I walked to the bottom of the valley
where the light didn't reach and it was very hot
like in a well of fire
where I wanted to forget what I could not
what I could only lay to rest in the caverns
facing Mount Zion that stands firm

No one here forgets anything

The meadows bleed like wet walls in a scaly house
where yellowed plaster flakes along the tiles' edge
Can life burst forth from a stump?
6000 houses
6000 windows
6000 jugs of bitterness
In desolate places I have given birth to straw
and the shepherd's speech has fallen silent
And yet it rains, has stormed, a lot, enough
to graze flocks in the wilderness
At night, green lights dot the opaque valley
facing Mount Zion that cannot be moved

Everyone here waits for a version of redemption

Archaeology

Empty-handed I return from the rich man's field
again, the moon stands high over Yaffa Street

Shabbat is over, shutters are pushed up
again, the air is filled with jasmine scent

Today, my songs have fallen silent

Like an exhausted prophet in a purple valley
I am haunted by an unspoken truth

A spoon swirls in a tea glass, inside a gutted house
on a one-way street that runs in two directions

How can I write about date-palms again
their shadows measuring the hours of the sun
reminding me I was not chosen?

From where will redemption come
in this city, where the Gate of Mercy is walled up?

Regret engraved in every stone
tangible, like the re-erected columns in the Cardo
that were found when we returned

Roman ruins, preservers of our past

Between the ground levels then and now
between layers of lust and yearning
shop-keepers call out to customers

Between white-golden dawns and orange sunsets
in royal blue damask nights
I keep unearthing, keep believing. I want my portion

Ein Kerem

after "In This Valley" by Yehuda Amichai

The road winds down into the valley
a valley like many here

carved out by many waters in endless years
with sudden breezes and instant stillness

valleys I have seen in the poems of Yehuda Amichai
poems that give words to speechlessness

that honor what was and was not
the in-betweens, like a breeze passing through the valley

without being destined for it
The day is hot, from the hills

I hear voices of men, machines wrecking
To my right, a building stretches into the void

over pines and umber soil, like his name
a pledge to choose life

There are loves that must die in their place and their time
He died in the building on the crest to my left

At Miriam's spring, naked children yell and splash water
in exhilaration, like only young children can
or truly happy people

I enter the garden alone, a sudden breeze
turns stillness into bouncing shadows
cools the sweat on my temples, my scorched words

In this valley, I want to sing of loves enduring
I want to leave the wrecked buildings of my life behind

Pico Boulevard

Pico Boulevard, the silence of a Saturday
sun bears down
on billboards that praise lawyers and movies
weed in the curb
Crows swagger, pick on scattered dates
in the grassy shadow of a swaying palm tree
in the hills
succulents cower on cardboard ridges
faithful like the olive tree
paper mansions cling to land not theirs
earth that might quake and swallow
eject and dispossess them
flimsy inheritance that captivates
the bygone scent of oranges
On this day in my tanned august glory
I do not worry, do not plead
I do not covet, do not crave
The cistern that I hew is full enough, my stride
still young, my china on the bottom shelf

Date Harvest

The season of the dates begins when the sun hovers
on this exact position in the morning
fills my balcony and living room
luminous shadows
most high
the brightness of my arrival one year ago
when everything seemed possible
when I was surely filled with the beauty
of this place
the sun a scarlet ball behind the trees
a grayish sky heralding heat
late in August

You began to leave my life
while the days grew longer
while the dates ripened
invisible, then green, now orange
dripping on the parking lot
squashed, such waste
for just one night

I will never think of dates the same again
of you, in the dry heat of the I-10
at the plantation store

How elusive it all seems
in brimming light, a bitter sound
dates falling to the ground

Memories of California

How fair are your tents, California, how fair
your marine layers lingering
in silent canyons until they evaporate
into the sharpness of your afternoons
every mountain crevice an eternity

How good your shoreline, a gentle curve and dunes
a stretch of wilderness where sea and desert merge
I miss your sand on my ankles, on my car seat
my laughter and my sunglasses
your sacred names, my dwelling place
the jewel on my windowsill

I miss your scent of herbs, your yellow flowers
brown-green shades of succulents
the chill at dusk a whisper and then calm

I miss you, California, I hear the wind
whipping through strawberry fields, seals calling
across the bay, the new moon is invisible
behind the cliff, dark waves are rising

How far I had to go, how far are now
your shining piers and your abundance
your creeks and scenic routes
submersed and clogged in fog

California Peaches

It's a good year for peaches, the first in many
another proof for having reached
the promised land
a tote full of peaches
warm velvet skin
yellow orange softness
Having lived just a tad more than half my life
the answer to suffering is *I don't know*—
this morning at the farmer's market
tasting peaches, I am redeemed
Sun tickles my bare legs and shoulders
and the ocean beckons
a hot day ahead
on the beaches in the Palisades
that westward facing stretch of earth
lined by a coastal highway
as the beach in Carcavelos
where thirty years ago
peach juice ran down our chins and wrists
the taste of velvet, salt and sunscreen
our skin smoother than the smoothest peach
and I was so in love with Vasco
Days of thundering waves and glaring sunlight
his curls peeked from beneath his helmet
the Marginal winding with the river widening
spending itself into the ocean, receiving

Santa Ana

A blue day, the sky is clear, beach littered
with shattered palm fronds, otherwise it's
empty, emptier even than on Christmas
or Thanksgiving Day

In the curb, wind-tossed carcasses
the loss unmeasured, inconceivable
now that the sun is back—
three days that feel like years

In the mist behind the pier smolders
a barred route to freedom. Where young women
rode on horseback to the grocery-store
waves lick up a smoldering shore
chimneys are survivors, tombstones—

Beyond the ridge, visible only on the map
hissing devils creep through canyons, deep
beneath brush and chaparral, uncontained
ecstatic in the breeze

When the sun sets the hills blaze up
now you can see it, from the freeway
from the bedroom window
north, east, west
a grapefruit glow throughout the night
a ring of godless pillars

The bird shrieks, alarmed
singed palm trees shiver
Santa Ana has come to town

Lines

Days have been foggy, a fog so thick
it blurs the rays from the streetlamps
When the temperature drops during the night, sometimes
I smell bonfire, or is it the smell of coal
like in Berlin winter nights many years ago

How west coast it felt, on our road trip to Mendocino
to sit around a fire pit in fleece and flip-flops
guitar, burgundy leaves and evergreens
sturdy trees bent halfway, resisting, yielding
to the Pacific wind

Another foggy morning, oil pumps slowly digging
rising in the swamps
and the magnolias in bloom, again
Each morning this week, as I drove north
the fog lifted around the curve before the exit
I wonder how many times
you have taken this same curve and exit
seen these same hills and scrubs
I still write poems to you, or rather
fragments, lines
or maybe they are messages to nobody and everyone

When I drove back home from the hospital today
I drove by the house where you once lived
It's boarded up now, *demolition notice*

On the east side one evening, I wanted to find
the place where my dead friend lived
I remembered a ramp, an underpass, a steep street
then left
or maybe right
past a low, white public building
lemon trees outside his kitchen window

I didn't know the address, I didn't find the place

In Hebrew angel means messenger and it does in English, too
City of Messengers, lonely city, vacant city
at night, the freeway free like in a Bruce Springsteen song
I wonder if LA wants to be loved or is unfazed
by the idea that it can disappear, like that
leaving but tar and marsh and desert wind
echoing from the hills

Have you noticed that there is no wind on foggy days?
In brisk sunshine, it is relentless

When I drove back home from the hospital today
I thought of the woman I had visited
whether she might read this week's Torah portion
Toledot: These are the lines of Isaac
I liked the woman's turquoise ring, from Santa Fe
where she went once with her husband, a jeweler
I want to go home to my garden, she said

I thought of the parents who lost their child
I met them in what for them is now the time *before*

I thought of the Mexican woman in the sauna
telling her friend that every day, she cries
Lloro, lloro, todos los días
but con 20 dólares in her pocket, ay
she feels as if she owns the world

It's been a while since I sauntered along peach-bowl freeways
with twenty dollars in my pocket
or balanced on the curb like on a tightrope
singing *It's only a Paper Moon*
I still confuse the Aramaic words for here and now

Last night I drove through a glen and up a hill
the palm trees were majestic
The rabbis knew that thoroughfares separate domains
yet the fog was as thick as everywhere

I turned the heating on
I watched the cone of light cut through the dark
like when I rode in my father's car
through the Black Forest in snow-filled nights

Snow Day

I left the bar while the music was playing
and walked to the subway at Union Square.

I didn't want to leave Manhattan,
I never want to leave Manhattan on the eve of a storm.

I wanted to walk through the night with you
until snowflakes appeared in the sky.

I wanted to wake up in your arms,
knowing that outside the snow piled up high

that we had all day to make love
that we could get up and walk through quiet streets.

There's nothing more romantic than snow in New York
I would say, and you wouldn't mind that it sounded trite.

I would compare the buildings on Fifth Avenue to mountains
on the horizon and tell you that I sometimes miss the Alps

yes, really, more than anything, I miss the Alps.

Maybe you would take my gloved hand
and with a few seconds delay, I would look at you.

I woke up in my Brooklyn apartment.
I heard my neighbors shovel and their children play.

The snow piled up high on the fence and my bike.
I texted the landlord to turn on the heat.

I wrote a poem, then went for a walk.
I missed the Alps and couldn't tell anyone.

Sunset Boulevard

We were friends of the same friend who hadn't seen each other in ten years. Over the past three days, time had contracted. We drove down from Los Feliz all dressed in black and took a right turn into the afternoon light. You can't come to Los Angeles and not have at least some fun, Christa said, and DJ let me smoke a cigarette inside the car. I leaned back like maybe a movie star would and blew the smoke out through the open sun top into the gentle March air, toward the famous palm trees, and I thought how normal and quiet Los Angeles looked, how airy and pretty, these famous low, white buildings. My skirt squeezed my empty stomach, and my blouse looked washed out and saggy. We talked again about the summer when we had first met, we discussed once more our friend's ex-lovers and what had gone wrong with the mother of his son, we shared gossip and anecdotes past the Viper Room and the Whiskey a Go Go and through the Dead Man's Curve as if all these stories were proof that he was still alive. The colorful wreaths in the trunk smelled heavy in their intense turquoise, yellow, pink, and orange, glaring like icing colors, so many flowers, so much green and wisdom and wealth along this former cattle trail. We wanted to send the wreaths out into the ocean, a ritual supposed to give meaning, three figures dressed in black at sunset on a beach watching two colorful wreaths floating, swallowed by the waves, floating, but we couldn't find a beach where we would be unobserved, sending out wreaths to God knows where in memory of the dead is forbidden without a proper permit, plus my plane was leaving in a few hours and we still needed to eat.

The Santa Monica pier shimmered silver as we veered back on whatever freeway DJ and Christa thought might be least clogged and had dinner somewhere near the airport. Everyone stared at us furtively, we were untouchables in the lit center of the restaurant with its open glass doors and heaters on the terrace, we drank fast and ate little and laughed loudly, dressed in black, tired, out of time, and then we raced to the airport, past the sparkling refinery that DJ had pointed out to me when he had picked me up three days earlier, the refinery where our friend had often filmed commercials, and I thought of Bruce Springsteen and one summer in another century, and then I cut the line at security by pointing to my clothes, mumbling something about a funeral and feeling guilty about it, but it did help me reach the gate when they were about to close it, and the moment I sat down in my aisle seat I fell into an empty sleep and didn't wake up until the plane touched ground in New York, where the A/C was blasting, my suitcase was missing, and it was snowing.

Also I Return

Maybe this is how life will be: a little room and a twin bed
an open suitcase, a haven for a while—
The plant that overlooks Bedford once was mine
it has grown in my friend's care, my friend who said
when she walked up the stoop
she saw the lamp was on and knew that I was home.

Down in Sunset Park, I had a little room for guests to stay
and overlook the yard, morning glories, fireflies—
In my old neighbors' garden, we sit under a red umbrella
the linden tree has grown two more years.
No, I say, we don't have fireflies in the desert wind.
The Brooklyn air is thick like a cocoon
it gets dark later in the east.

In summer, my mother liked to sit outside and watch the dusk
turn blue, much later still than now,
her arms were warm, a yellow blanket.
Todd and Regina wave into the night.

At the corner of the block is a new hotel
where my parents will never stay.
They won't walk down 4th Avenue again
to take "the orange line"—4th Avenue
where my dad bought flowers for my birthday
at Bodega El Centennial.
They won't come out to California, either
the flight too burdensome for their old age.

And granted, how easy to forget
driving up the crisp Pacific coast
a European continent
or even Brooklyn with its parks and ferries—
how easy to remember now that once, all this was mine.

Leaving New York V

I was not there when you woke up
under light sheets and busy fans
It's been humid where you are

The linden tree outside your window
has grown another year
I knew its bed barren, cracked earth and dog pee
How fast it grew

Where I live now
I came in time to know the Ralph's on Beverly
that since has closed
After 12 months we count as locals

After 20 years of growth
a cactus is still smaller than a tree
I remember huge cacti in the Sonora desert
years before I knew you
my shadow flickering across sun-burnt soil
with the train's silhouette

I was not there when you returned to life and fell
into the sweaty arms of those who stayed
who bask with you now, along
your shores and rivers, in parks and squares
where I, too, once walked embraced by you
a key to your apartment in my hand

Montauk Point

I have been here before we arrived, I know
the smell of salt seeped into walls and floors,
summers never erased by air-conditioning,
white cupboards and lined shelves, mowed grass
the sky at noon—
I slip barefoot through many doors and curtains
the sunlight between the ocean and the bay.
Later, fractured rays fall on polished skin,
the thicket of my hair, toned arms. Waves behind my eyes.
Damp towels waft like pines outside the kitchen windows,
hydrangeas, gleaming oak leaves.
The earth spins through the stars. An orange moon rises.

Double Eye

I walked by the coffee shop today and saw you sitting there on the stairs. You were wearing your new hat and glasses. You always wear glasses instead of lenses on flight days. Nobody paid attention to you, squeezed in between a flower bucket and your backpack, reading a non-fiction bestseller. You looked young and fragile that morning, almost ethereal. You didn't notice when I crossed the street and sat down beside you. I leaned back against the clammy limestone wall and watched your fingers turn the pages. I have always enjoyed beholding the evenness of your lineaments; delicate antagonists of your inner fractures. We were both waiting for me. When I finally arrived, you stood up and walked toward me. You left the book on top of your backpack, but I couldn't read the words. All I saw were blurry letters, and the harder I tried to seize them, the blurrier they got. I observed the two of us absorbed in our embrace, amidst a casually dispersed coffee-drinking crowd. My heart was beating fast against your chest and as I recognized the smell of your skin I wondered whether you never wear fragrances or just not on flight days. I have remained here on the stairs for the rest of the day. At June's patient and idle pace, the sun sauntered across the opposite sidewalk until it lasciviously climbed up the facades and eventually fell off the roofs into the wide, northeastern sky.

Kenneth Hahn Park

The sunlight in my hair is beautiful
his voice as tender as his fingertips, clear
and elusive, as the waning rays on a plane's rudder

above us on its flight to somewhere in the east
for summer has passed and the rains must come.

The sun is slowly crawling into canyons
a topaz haze, a silent reckoning. Earth and grass
a womb-shaped meadow, a monument to sunken dreams.

Oil pumps bend. In the distance, waves wash ashore
and reach for stars and sand
recede and leave a trail of foam and pebbles
faint and dazzled

our eyes like doves
our shadows as short as seven years
inscribed in chronicles of days better than wine

rare shards of pottery, sapphires gleaming
on a tel of verdant pastures

my inland empire
a broken dam, a locked garden.

A Zimmer in the Forest

Behind olive trees and pines, a white light calls as the air
cools down and shadows fall on treetops that linger
in the sun, on stones and terracotta soil
The storm of light-dark green and citrus-yellow
that has engulfed me all day calms down
poppies close their petals—
Later, Adi and I walk through the moshav
together with most of her children
Tefila has long begun
when she points to where the white light from before
has turned into stripes of orange, red, and purple
What a sunset, she says, and the four-year-old
stumbles and cries
the baby in the stroller looks surprised and her brother
picks up his kippa as a car is passing by
and I hear men singing in the Beit Midrash like
we will sing around the table, a new song
Come into my garden, bloom, my vine
and as I take in one more glance
I think I see, as if painted by Chagall
the rabbis from Tiberias, wrapped
in their most splendid garments, floating
over the valley that sinks into a velvet night

Tu BiShevat in the Arava

A sudden wind hurls down Route 90
a flash flood rushing through a wadi
a voice paving a highway through the wilderness

The morning's blue dissolves with the full moon
clouds from the west hide the sun

In the east, the contours of the mountains
are invisible, their shades of red and brown
their crevices and veins, patches of beige

Date palms cry out, a green sea in distress

Army barracks espouse the earth
hold on to her, claim inheritance

Dust of camels, scent of frankincense

A howling scatters branches across fleeting sands
I wait for the wind to settle, a harbinger of old

Caravans from Sheba, dhaus from Zanzibar

Before the planting, I sweep
red, brown and beige soil from marbled tiles

Barefoot, I scout the horizon
for the next decade to emerge from the peninsula

To Proclaim Freedom

Petra lies concealed by mountains
Aqaba across the water, in sight
but out of reach.

The arrival of a day of comfort
is among seven matters not known to man
and three come unawares:
Moshiach, a found object, and a scorpion.

A long-distance phone call around midnight
does not bring redemption but truths foreseen,
an unexpected freedom.

Route 12 winds past the Red Canyon
and army bases, beige brown black rocks.

The wadi near my house
is an ancient route to Mecca, a shortcut to the beach.
Gravels crunch, a fly is whirring, my heart beats.
In the wind, palm fronds confront the sea
like a woman's hair without a scarf.

Behind the fence snaking across hilltops
I see Egypt and I know that somewhere in the mist
begins Arabia.

Beyond the mountains, Petra
across the water, Aqaba—

I rest on faded rugs, pink-yellow cushions
sap drips on my skin
out of a green-turquoise expanse.

I swim with fish, giddy and astonished
to share their silent world again,
bubbles rise in pillars of light.

Before his death, Jacob promised to foretell
what will happen in the end of days
but divine vision left his eyes and all he had to offer
was poetry, and blessings—
secrets that remain unseen, an unexpected peace

Hiatus in the Sinai

I do not go near the mountain hidden by ragged summits the color of all sands, inlaid with green and red. Yesterday, a fluorescent ball lingered in a sky of dust. It was the sun, not the moon; Shavuot has not yet passed, our undefined defining moment that happened, as some say, on a volcano across the shallow sea. Even T-Mobile can't decide whether I am in Egypt or Arabia

I live in Los Angeles, I tell the innkeeper who claims I look like I am from here, the Sinai. Right, I say, and aren't we all, I think, like the Apiru, who covered huts with palm fronds and roamed this maze of rocks and dust and sand, handsome, maybe, as the men who flash smiles at me with their mustaches. I do know how to dress for desert lands

The cats of Egypt are more attached and more demanding than their cousins in Jerusalem. I can't chase them away, like the locals do or folks from the kibbutz up north; I caress the black one who walked out of an ancient tableau to bring me luck

Are you a daughter of Jerusalem, asked the man in the gift shop at the Bible Lands Museum and I said, "I am tonight!" When I keep my Hebrew short, gestures precise, I pass. In one unfathomable week from now, I will re-enter the land and return to the diaspora

The wind today, I can't see the other side, Arabia, hidden by foam and spray. The instructor squints across the water; I wonder if the dive will happen or if I will see the corals as I have seen the mountain, from afar

Song at the Sea

I live in Venice now, not far from Kinney's gondolas
I can't see the ocean; I know it's near
the light is brilliant
especially after the rain
It has rained a lot these days
I have crossed saltmarsh and concrete swamps
I have miracles left inside
the sound from distant nights in Palestine
I would have made a fine pioneer
on the threshing floor, under the moon

I live in Venice now, I cross canals
I can't see the hills; the land is low
the sky is misty
Dean Martin swooning in my ear
about the pyramids along the Nile
asking that I let him go

The beach is gray, ever gentle on my mind
Someone's watching from the lifeguard tower
someone who would do, not want, the best for me

I live in the tropics now, I watch the sun rise
the cockatoo sings loud at dusk
every day is candle-lighting time
I walk past pastel bungalows
the sky is violet and dark soft blue
the palms' green lit up by a cosmic bounce

Remember the Land

From a windowsill in Yemin Moshe, a red lamp
shines into the night of my departure
before dawn
the muezzins' calls wash up the slopes in waves,
sunlight falls into the emptiness that was my home

In the synagogue next door, men and their voices
rise in prayer while the garbage man drags
a bag stuffed with remnants
from a new life suddenly on halt
over cobblestones and the cat with turquoise eyes
who hoped to be adopted, prowls past my locked door
his tail wagging, its tip balancing
around the corner to the Rav Itzhak Badhav stairs

The bells of Mount Zion proclaim
my accumulating absence with every quarter
of an hour and crows hop through the fountain
in Bloomfield Garden as they did
in my early poems
when I was the same and someone else—

Will the hills remember my steps
the wall miss my palms
will the air retain my laughter
my cries and songs?

How tall will my friend's children grow until I return
from my unwritten years
my other halted life in this Pacific desert dwelling
where a green light shines behind the date palm
east of La Cienega?

Under the Sun, Exactly

On the beach in Santa Monica, my suede boots
peek into the frame, tips perked up, black jeans
the glistening breezy sea
I captured all that five years ago, today

boots and jeans are different, although
they almost look the same, as does
the ocean, although my camera roll claims
nothing is new under this sky, precisely

this different sky, long ago reflected in the windows
of Joan Didion's bungalow in Malibu, my first
reckoning of the far west as *plausible,* before I
commuted once a week to Calabasas, before my
dead lover's teenage son played ukulele
west of the 1, on Instagram, his California

child, ginger curls against a pomegranate sky
wooden power poles and purple headlights
the curved mountain silhouette, lifelines

like canyons. The winds from Santa Ana never
are as hot as I imagined them. Tonight

they rouse palm fronds that bend gracefully
against a waning moon and blurry streetlights
stoic ballerinas in silent, velvet sacredness. Some

fall on driveways and sidewalks, into the canals
where they will languish, under the sun
exactly, prehistoric pelvises, prickly, dry
hollow and heavy all at once

Prophecy Ceased

And then prophecy ceased
palm fronds continued to quiver, the wind to blow
across coastal plains, swamps and tar pits
and the ocean
like pelicans darting above crests of waves
seagulls hovering over the expanse

Prophecy ceased
all utterances had been uttered
future dispersions were to be
unannounced echoes of what already happened
Great rivers had swept the land
now, the old tunnel would once again
haul water from the Pool of Siloam

Prophecy ceased
geckos continued to bask on split-up rocks and the scent
of eucalyptus, thyme, and lilac to fill the air
crisp, and with a hint of chill
bearing down on searing valleys, shaded glens

Prophecy ceased
the sun sent silvery copper signals
from the hills in twilight hours, as before
and I turned to you

You were standing
barefoot on terra cotta ashes
near the olive grove, the henna bushes
a loose end of your scarf flapping, and your fringes
Sand on your lips, and mine
I placed my right palm on your shoulder

I Am Talking to You Now

The rug was royal blue and desert yellow,
hard wool pricked my skin.
Humid light seeped gray through open windows,
the radio had been playing through the night.

The little day, they call this hour in French
I said when you walked me to the station,
past the pastry bakery, dew on the lawn.
You smiled, your arm around my shoulder.

From the train, through sepia windowpanes
I saw you standing on the platform,
then turned my head and waved.
The leather seats were burgundy.

On foggy afternoons, we walked the dog
then lay on your twin bed and listened
to cassette tapes.
You always chose the tunes.
I didn't mind,
you were bothered by compliancy.

One night, your curls around my fingers,
I saw our shadows on the wall
and knew I would remember this forever.

I don't speak of you as often as I used to.
In the sea breeze hover words you said,
some quieter and some louder—
Talk to me, Julia, why don't you talk to me?

Mount Royal

for Leonard Cohen

I played your music for all the men I knew.
Here I was, alone.
I came empty-handed,
I placed an acorn on your headstone.
There was a lot of snow in gelid sunshine,
I was lucky to find the acorn.
I placed it on your headstone, a shy caress.

At twelve on my windowsill, I listened
to your voice on my mother's record album,
reading what I learned were *liner notes*.
Twelve short paragraphs unlocked your world for me.
We would have disagreed. I don't worship easily.

One summer afternoon in a college town,
the dean of sacred Latin
surprised his son and me and asked
about the sultry music we were playing.
It never occurred to me to call your music sultry,
my tolerance is high for heat and humidity;
you were profound
in your distaste for bigotry.

You led the way; you walked behind me.
You may have never thought of me again,
awe-struck young woman from Berlin—
one day in March you looked at me, engrossed.

I played your music for all the men I knew.
Here I was, alone.
I came empty-handed,
I placed an acorn on your headstone.
I washed my eyelids with the snow around your grave.

Ascent

The fog reached far during the night
by Sunset it burns off
herbs and pinecones, a still small breeze
heat waiting in the shadow
together with the stags
heat that crushes under feet
crackling silence
the tempting fragrance of the chaparral
dust and sweat and laundered shirt

*

Shaded love streets, lifelines
connecting two domains
since time immemorial
people know where to traverse
from the narrows to the sun
greeted by cypress, palm and eucalyptus tree
on the ledge
Mulholland a karmelit
Holy mountains, hills of saints
strung like pearls around basin and valley

*

My singing heart sits shiva in advance
like God over the world before the flood
No photo will preserve the essence
the serenity I feel
under this ungraspable wide sky
One thing I ask
to never have to leave this canopy
to dwell in this beauty all my life
Let this be my inheritance

Notes

Heiligenberg (Holy Mountain) and Königsstuhl King's Seat) are two mountains flanking the German city of Heidelberg.

"Rehov HaMevaser" translates to "Street of the Herald."

Tammuz is a summer month on the Jewish calendar.

The epigraph to "Praia Grande" is from the poem "Ternura" (Tenderness) by David Mourão-Ferreira and translates to "After the sun, there is nothing else."

The poem "Ein Kerem" quotes lines from Yehuda Amichai's poem "In This Valley."

The title "Also I Return" is taken from Walt Whitman's poem "Crossing Brooklyn Ferry."

The epigraph for "Hippocampus Is Latin for Seahorse" is a quote from Christine Blasey Ford's testimony against then Supreme Court nominee, Brett Kavanaugh.

Tu BiShevat is a Jewish holiday celebrating the new year for the trees.

The line in "Under the Sun, Exactly" (after a song by Serge Gainsbourg) calling the west "plausible" is an echo of Joan Didion's essay "Goodbye to All That" in which she described New York as a "plausible" place.

"Double Eye" is the name of a coffee bar in Berlin-Schöneberg.

Karmelit is a term from Jewish law referring to a space that belongs to both public and private domains.

Thank You

I am grateful to the thoughtful editors at Kelsay Books for giving this book a home as well as to Dan Alter, Rachel Kaufman, Carine Topal, and David L. Ulin for taking the time to read the manuscript and write favorable blurbs.

About the Author

Julia Knobloch received rabbinic ordination from Hebrew Union College in Los Angeles and lives in San Pedro, California. Her previous poetry collections are *Book of Failed Salvation* (Ben Yehuda Press, 2021) and *Do not Return* (Broadstone Books, 2019).

www.ingramcontent.com/pod-product-compliance
Lightning Source LLC
Chambersburg PA
CBHW022146160426
43197CB00009B/1443